National Parks

2026 WEEKLY PLANNER

JULY 2025–DECEMBER 2026

ROCK
POINT

2026 YEAR AT A GLANCE

JANUARY

S	M	T	W	T	F	S
				1	2	3
4	5	6	7	8	9	10
11	12	13	14	15	16	17
18	19	20	21	22	23	24
25	26	27	28	29	30	31

FEBRUARY

S	M	T	W	T	F	S
1	2	3	4	5	6	7
8	9	10	11	12	13	14
15	16	17	18	19	20	21
22	23	24	25	26	27	28

MARCH

S	M	T	W	T	F	S
1	2	3	4	5	6	7
8	9	10	11	12	13	14
15	16	17	18	19	20	21
22	23	24	25	26	27	28
29	30	31				

APRIL

S	M	T	W	T	F	S
			1	2	3	4
5	6	7	8	9	10	11
12	13	14	15	16	17	18
19	20	21	22	23	24	25
26	27	28	29	30		

MAY

S	M	T	W	T	F	S
					1	2
3	4	5	6	7	8	9
10	11	12	13	14	15	16
17	18	19	20	21	22	23
24	25	26	27	28	29	30
31						

JUNE

S	M	T	W	T	F	S
	1	2	3	4	5	6
7	8	9	10	11	12	13
14	15	16	17	18	19	20
21	22	23	24	25	26	27
28	29	30				

JULY

S	M	T	W	T	F	S
			1	2	3	4
5	6	7	8	9	10	11
12	13	14	15	16	17	18
19	20	21	22	23	24	25
26	27	28	29	30	31	

AUGUST

S	M	T	W	T	F	S
						1
2	3	4	5	6	7	8
9	10	11	12	13	14	15
16	17	18	19	20	21	22
23	24	25	26	27	28	29
30	31					

SEPTEMBER

S	M	T	W	T	F	S
		1	2	3	4	5
6	7	8	9	10	11	12
13	14	15	16	17	18	19
20	21	22	23	24	25	26
27	28	29	30			

OCTOBER

S	M	T	W	T	F	S
				1	2	3
4	5	6	7	8	9	10
11	12	13	14	15	16	17
18	19	20	21	22	23	24
25	26	27	28	29	30	31

NOVEMBER

S	M	T	W	T	F	S
1	2	3	4	5	6	7
8	9	10	11	12	13	14
15	16	17	18	19	20	21
22	23	24	25	26	27	28
29	30					

DECEMBER

S	M	T	W	T	F	S
		1	2	3	4	5
6	7	8	9	10	11	12
13	14	15	16	17	18	19
20	21	22	23	24	25	26
27	28	29	30	31		

2027 YEAR AT A GLANCE

JANUARY

S	M	T	W	T	F	S
					1	2
3	4	5	6	7	8	9
10	11	12	13	14	15	16
17	18	19	20	21	22	23
24	25	26	27	28	29	30
31						

FEBRUARY

S	M	T	W	T	F	S
	1	2	3	4	5	6
7	8	9	10	11	12	13
14	15	16	17	18	19	20
21	22	23	24	25	26	27
28						

MARCH

S	M	T	W	T	F	S
	1	2	3	4	5	6
7	8	9	10	11	12	13
14	15	16	17	18	19	20
21	22	23	24	25	26	27
28	29	30	31			

APRIL

S	M	T	W	T	F	S
				1	2	3
4	5	6	7	8	9	10
11	12	13	14	15	16	17
18	19	20	21	22	23	24
25	26	27	28	29	30	

MAY

S	M	T	W	T	F	S
						1
2	3	4	5	6	7	8
9	10	11	12	13	14	15
16	17	18	19	20	21	22
23	24	25	26	27	28	29
30	31					

JUNE

S	M	T	W	T	F	S
		1	2	3	4	5
6	7	8	9	10	11	12
13	14	15	16	17	18	19
20	21	22	23	24	25	26
27	28	29	30			

JULY

S	M	T	W	T	F	S
				1	2	3
4	5	6	7	8	9	10
11	12	13	14	15	16	17
18	19	20	21	22	23	24
25	26	27	28	29	30	31

AUGUST

S	M	T	W	T	F	S
1	2	3	4	5	6	7
8	9	10	11	12	13	14
15	16	17	18	19	20	21
22	23	24	25	26	27	28
29	30	31				

SEPTEMBER

S	M	T	W	T	F	S
			1	2	3	4
5	6	7	8	9	10	11
12	13	14	15	16	17	18
19	20	21	22	23	24	25
26	27	28	29	30		

OCTOBER

S	M	T	W	T	F	S
					1	2
3	4	5	6	7	8	9
10	11	12	13	14	15	16
17	18	19	20	21	22	23
24	25	26	27	28	29	30
31						

NOVEMBER

S	M	T	W	T	F	S
	1	2	3	4	5	6
7	8	9	10	11	12	13
14	15	16	17	18	19	20
21	22	23	24	25	26	27
28	29	30				

DECEMBER

S	M	T	W	T	F	S
			1	2	3	4
5	6	7	8	9	10	11
12	13	14	15	16	17	18
19	20	21	22	23	24	25
26	27	28	29	30	31	

JULY
Lassen Volcanic National Park

Open 24 hours a day, 365 days a year, Lassen Volcanic National Park is the perfect location for backcountry hikers, outdoor enthusiasts, and winter recreationists. In 1972, the park became designated wilderness of the National Wilderness Preservation System. Not only is it home to steaming fumaroles, wildflower meadows, clear mountain lakes, and volcanoes, this national park is the spot to go no matter the season. In the winter, go sledding, snowshoeing, cross-country skiing, and snowboarding. Then, when the weather turns to spring and summer, find a great selection of activities such as ranger-led programs, field seminars,

auto touring, and backpacking. While you're there, head over to Manzanita Lake with its expansive campground and museum—and for a brilliant view of the 10,457-foot Lassen Peak. The jagged peaks of Lassen Volcanic National Park represent its eruptive past. The park is also known as the largest hydrothermal area, so dress appropriately as you hike by steam and volcanic gas vents, boiling mud pots, and vivid turquoise pools. Your stories of traveling either Bumpass Hell Trail or Devil's Kitchen Trail will be ones you share for years to come.

JULY 2025

NOTES	SUNDAY	MONDAY	TUESDAY
			1 CANADA DAY (CAN)
	6	**7**	**8**
	13	**14**	**15**
	20	**21**	**22**
	27	**28**	**29**

JULY 2025

WEDNESDAY	THURSDAY	FRIDAY	SATURDAY
◗ 2	3	4	5
		INDEPENDENCE DAY (US)	
9 ●	10	11	12
16	17 ◖	18	19
23 ○	24	25	26
30	31		

LASSEN VOLCANIC NATIONAL PARK

LOCATION: Northern California, approximately 3 hours NE of Sacramento

SIZE: 106,452 acres

BEST TIME TO VISIT: July through September

NATURE: The park boasts more than 700 flowering plant species such as sugar pine, common wildflowers, red fir, pinemat manzanita, whitebark pine, and mountain hemlock.

HABITATS: Lassen is home to approximately 300 species of vertebrates including the black bear, Sierra Nevada red fox, mountain lion, and snowshoe hare.

ACTIVITIES: Auto touring, biking, boating, camping, fishing, hiking, horseback riding, picnicking, paddling, swimming, and winter recreations.

NATURAL FEATURES: Lake Helen, the Big Boiler (fumarole), Kings Creek Falls, Reflection Lake, Lassen Peak (the largest lava dome on Earth), Chaos Crags, and more!

MONDAY (JUNE)   **30**

TUESDAY CANADA DAY (CAN)   **1**

WEDNESDAY ▶   **2**

THURSDAY   **3**

FRIDAY INDEPENDENCE DAY (US)   **4**

SATURDAY   **5**

SUNDAY   **6**

JULY 2025

MONDAY   **7**

TUESDAY   **8**

WEDNESDAY   **9**

THURSDAY ●   **10**

FRIDAY 11

SATURDAY 12

SUNDAY 13

Manzanita Lake is barricaded by a rock avalanche with a trail that circles the lake. It is a favorite spot for photographers.

JULY 2025

MONDAY 14

TUESDAY 15

WEDNESDAY 16

THURSDAY 17

FRIDAY ☽ **18**

SATURDAY **19**

SUNDAY **20**

The 1915 eruption at Lassen Peak was the most powerful to occur in the Cascades before the 1980 eruption of Mount Saint Helens.

JULY 2025

MONDAY 21

TUESDAY 22

WEDNESDAY 23

THURSDAY ○ 24

FRIDAY

25

SATURDAY

26

SUNDAY

27

If you're highly sensitive to smells, stay away from Bumpass Hell Trail. The natural gases released from the mineral-rich water smells like rotten eggs, and will stay with you long after you leave.

AUGUST
Zion National Park

The complexity of Zion is impossible to capture in a photograph—it can only be truly understood by those who have stood between the sandstone canyon walls, felt the spray of waterfalls cascading into Emerald Pools, and seen the vibrant green of lush, hanging gardens. Zion National Park, established in 1919, is the center of the geological sequence of rock layers known as the Grand Staircase—its top rocks are the bottom rocks at Bryce Canyon, and the Grand Canyon's top rocks are Zion's bottom rocks. Around 7,000 years ago, nomadic Native American groups began passing through this intersection of the Colorado Plateau, Great Basin, and Mojave Desert; today the park sees more than five million visitors every year. It was a

barren, flat basin 240 million years ago, but erosion and sedimentation, combined with uplifting forces within the Earth's crust, created the extreme elevations we see today. Climb to the top of Mount Baldy by Observation Point Trail and get a stunning overlook of the park at 6,521 feet. Spend a morning hiking through the Narrows, an iconic narrow gorge with walls thousands of feet tall. This hike requires wading through the steep Virgin River, which drops an average of 71 feet per mile, so bring waterproof gear and stay cognizant of flash floods. For a less strenuous activity, drive through the Zion-Mount Carmel Tunnel, peeking through windows cut into the sandstone to see incredible views of this geologic paradise.

AUGUST 2025

NOTES	SUNDAY	MONDAY	TUESDAY
	3	4	5
		SUMMER BANK HOLIDAY (UK-SCT)	
	10	11	12
	17	18	19
	24	25	26
	31	SUMMER BANK HOLIDAY (UK-ENG/NIR/WAL)	

AUGUST 2025

WEDNESDAY	THURSDAY	FRIDAY	SATURDAY
		☽	1	2
6	7	8 ●	9
13	14	15 ☾	16
20	21	22 ○	23
27	28	29	30

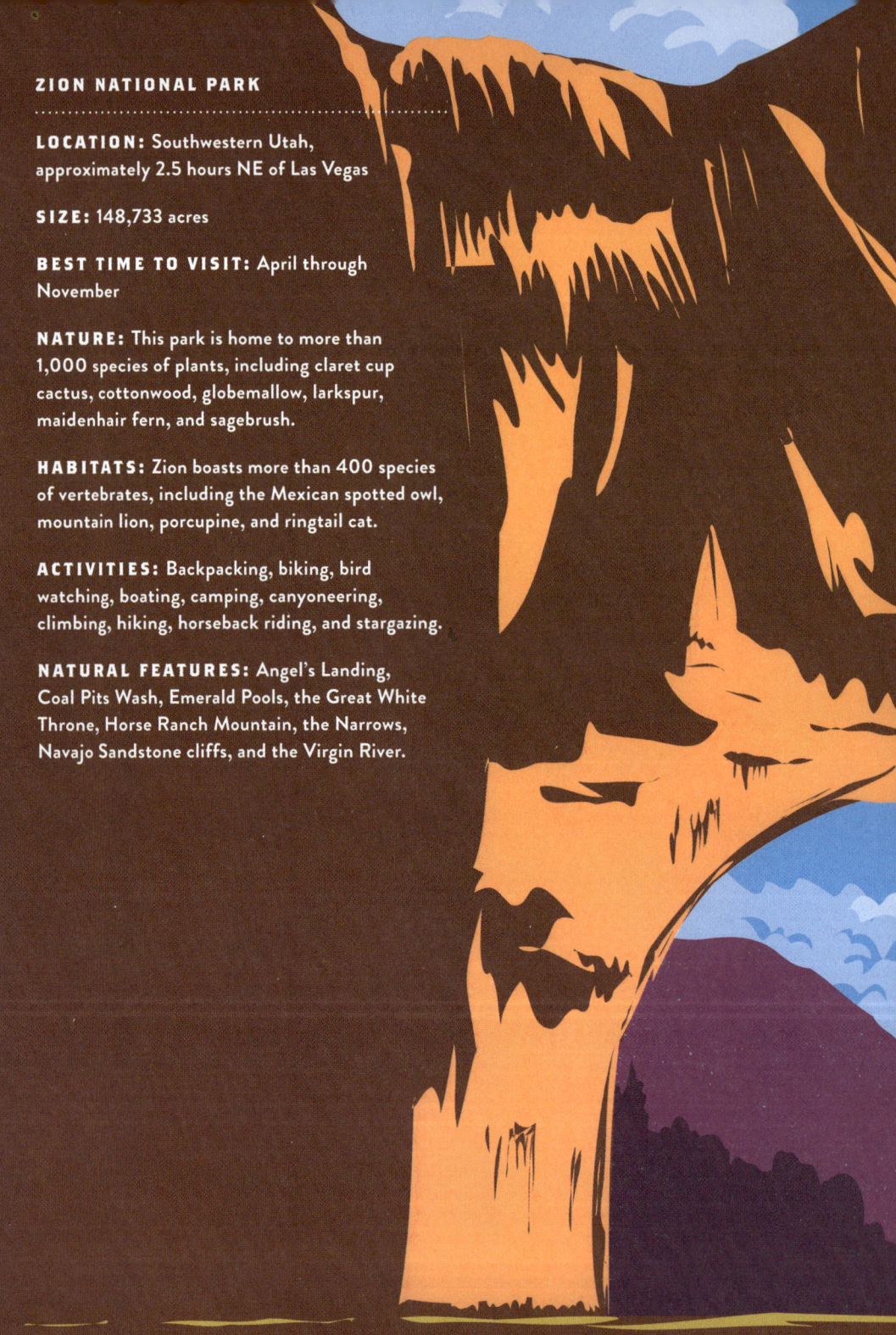

ZION NATIONAL PARK

LOCATION: Southwestern Utah, approximately 2.5 hours NE of Las Vegas

SIZE: 148,733 acres

BEST TIME TO VISIT: April through November

NATURE: This park is home to more than 1,000 species of plants, including claret cup cactus, cottonwood, globemallow, larkspur, maidenhair fern, and sagebrush.

HABITATS: Zion boasts more than 400 species of vertebrates, including the Mexican spotted owl, mountain lion, porcupine, and ringtail cat.

ACTIVITIES: Backpacking, biking, bird watching, boating, camping, canyoneering, climbing, hiking, horseback riding, and stargazing.

NATURAL FEATURES: Angel's Landing, Coal Pits Wash, Emerald Pools, the Great White Throne, Horse Ranch Mountain, the Narrows, Navajo Sandstone cliffs, and the Virgin River.

MONDAY (JULY)   **28**

TUESDAY (JULY)   **29**

WEDNESDAY (JULY)   **30**

THURSDAY (JULY)   **31**

FRIDAY ◗   **1**

SATURDAY   **2**

SUNDAY   **3**

AUGUST 2025

MONDAY SUMMER BANK HOLIDAY (UK-SCT)   **4**

TUESDAY   **5**

WEDNESDAY   **6**

THURSDAY   **7**

FRIDAY   **8**

SATURDAY ●   **9**

SUNDAY   **10**

Today, Zion National Park is home to about
20,000 wild turkeys, after the native population
disappeared and was reintroduced in the 1980s.

AUGUST 2025

MONDAY 11

TUESDAY 12

WEDNESDAY 13

THURSDAY 14

FRIDAY 15

SATURDAY ◑ 16

SUNDAY 17

At Zion Canyon's Weeping Rock, water takes more than 1,000 years to filter through the sandstone walls.

AUGUST 2025

MONDAY 18

TUESDAY 19

WEDNESDAY 20

THURSDAY 21

FRIDAY   **22**

SATURDAY ○   **23**

SUNDAY   **24**

In 2014, 26 bighorn sheep had to be airlifted out of Zion's desert due to their overwhelmingly abundant population.

AUGUST 2025

MONDAY SUMMER BANK HOLIDAY (UK-ENG/NIR/WAL)   **25**

TUESDAY   **26**

WEDNESDAY   **27**

THURSDAY   **28**

FRIDAY 29

SATURDAY 30

SUNDAY ☽ 31

The park was named by Mormon pioneers in the late 1800s. Zion means "refuge" or "sanctuary" in ancient Hebrew.

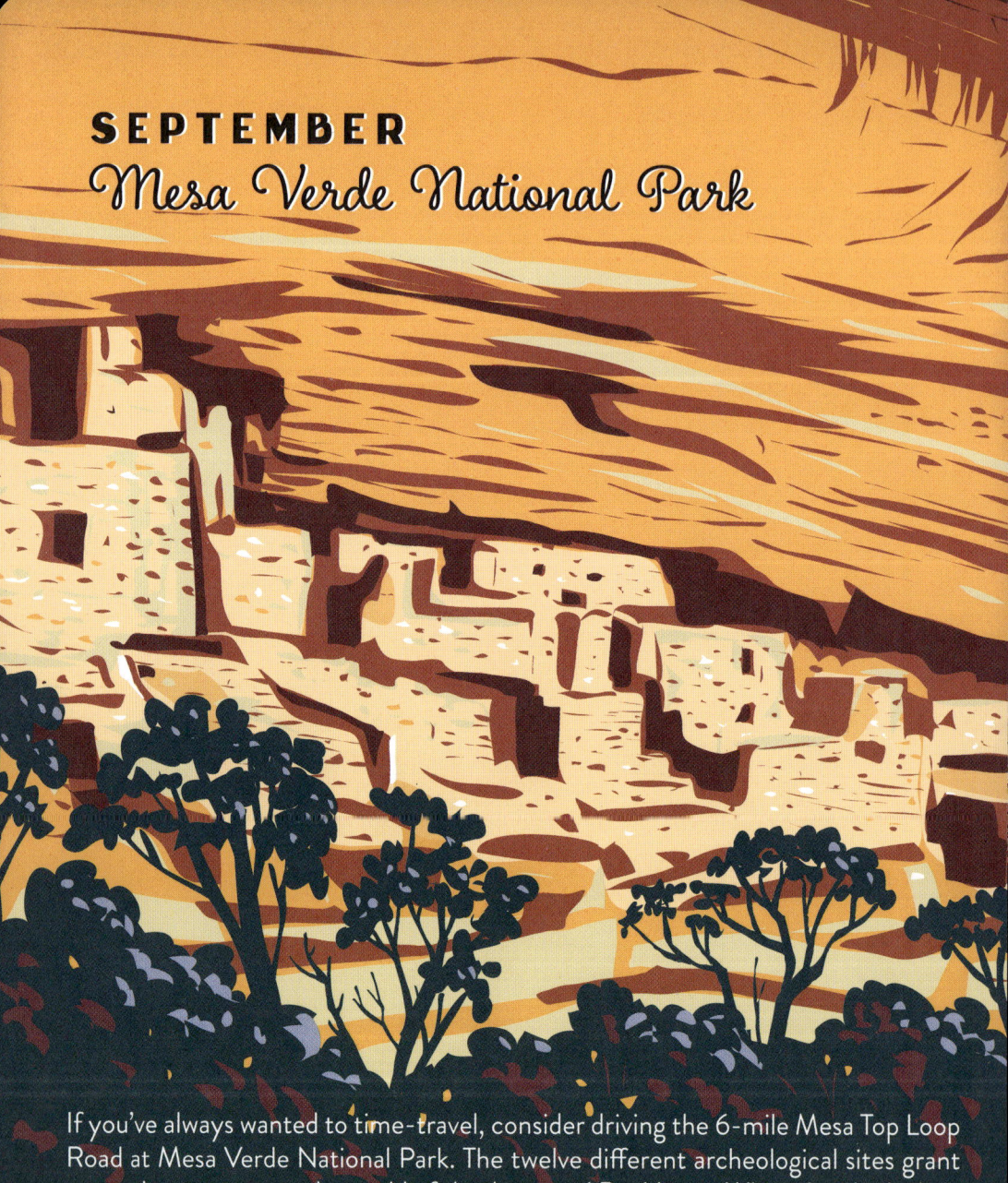

SEPTEMBER
Mesa Verde National Park

If you've always wanted to time-travel, consider driving the 6-mile Mesa Top Loop Road at Mesa Verde National Park. The twelve different archeological sites grant you a chance to enter the world of the Ancestral Puebloans. When they built their cliff dwellings throughout the 1200s, they could not have known the longevity or significance of their archeological impact. Mesa Verde National Park, established in 1906 by President Theodore Roosevelt, is a UNESCO World Heritage Site and home to more than 4,700 exceptionally preserved archeological sites, from Cliff Palace to Balcony House. Geologically, the semiarid park is less of a flat-topped

mesa and more of a cuesta, a ridge with a steep face on one side that gradually slopes toward the south, with cracks of canyons and rivers running through it. Take in the vastness of the park at Park Point Fire Lookout, a station made in 1939 to detect wildfires and the highest point in Mesa Verde. Hike the 2.4-mile Petroglyph Point Trail to appreciate early rock carvings or walk the half-mile Farming Terrace Trail to see where prehistoric check dams created space to farm corn. Make sure to bring plenty of water to cope with the heat and keep an eye out for desert wildlife such as turkey vultures and collared lizards.

SEPTEMBER 2025

NOTES	SUNDAY	MONDAY	TUESDAY
		1	**2**
		LABOR DAY (US) LABOUR DAY (CAN)	
	● **7**	**8**	**9**
	FATHER'S DAY (AUS/NZ) GRANDPARENTS' DAY (US)		
	◐ **14**	**15**	**16**
		FIRST DAY OF NATIONAL HISPANIC HERITAGE MONTH	
	21 ○	**22**	**23**
		FALL EQUINOX ROSH HASHANAH (BEGINS AT SUNDOWN)	
	28 ◑	**29**	**30**

SEPTEMBER 2025

WEDNESDAY	THURSDAY	FRIDAY	SATURDAY
3	4	5	6
10	11 PATRIOT DAY (US)	12	13
17	18	19	20
24	25	26	27

MESA VERDE NATIONAL PARK

LOCATION: Southwestern Colorado

SIZE: 52,485 acres

BEST TIME TO VISIT: May through October

NATURE: Mesa Verde boasts more than 640 species of plants, including Cliff Palace milkvetch, Mesa Verde stickseed, snowberry, skunkbush, Utah juniper, and rare Mesa Verde Wandering Aletes.

HABITATS: The park is home to approximately 300 species of vertebrates, including the black-chinned hummingbird, collared lizard, spotted bat, prairie rattlesnake, and wild turkey.

ACTIVITIES: Attending cultural demonstrations, bird watching, camping, hiking, photography, stargazing, touring cliff dwellings, and winter activities.

NATURAL FEATURES: Cliff Palace (the largest cliff dwelling in North America), the Mancos River, Montezuma Valley, Prater Ridge, Wetherill Mesa, and more!

SEPTEMBER

MONDAY LABOR DAY (US) / LABOUR DAY (CAN) 1

TUESDAY 2

WEDNESDAY 3

THURSDAY 4

FRIDAY 5

SATURDAY 6

SUNDAY FATHER'S DAY (AUS/NZ) / GRANDPARENTS' DAY (US) ● 7

SEPTEMBER 2025

MONDAY 8

TUESDAY 9

WEDNESDAY 10

THURSDAY PATRIOT DAY (US) 11

FRIDAY 12

SATURDAY 13

SUNDAY ◐ 14

Mesa Verde is part of the Four Corners Region, the only place in the country where four states (Colorado, Utah, New Mexico, and Arizona) come together.

SEPTEMBER 2025

MONDAY FIRST DAY OF NATIONAL HISPANIC HERITAGE MONTH **15**

TUESDAY **16**

WEDNESDAY **17**

THURSDAY **18**

FRIDAY

19

SATURDAY

20

SUNDAY

21

Since 1989, more than 36,000 acres of forests and shrublands have been destroyed by large-scale wildfires in Mesa Verde.

SEPTEMBER 2025

MONDAY FALL EQUINOX / ROSH HASHANAH (BEGINS AT SUNDOWN) ○

22

TUESDAY

23

WEDNESDAY

24

THURSDAY

25

FRIDAY 26

SATURDAY 27

SUNDAY 28

The reason why the Ancestral Puebloans left Mesa Verde in 1300 CE is a mystery. Experts believe it might have been a combination of drought and overpopulation, but we'll never truly know!

OCTOBER
Great Smoky Mountains National Park

Witness the towering mountains and magical, smoky haze of the Smokies—the tallest mountains in the Appalachian chain. Established in 1934, Great Smoky Mountains National Park is forested in a diverse array of green that transforms into a mosaic of red, orange, and yellow over the park's busy autumn months. Trek past groves of teaberry and rosebay rhododendron to Rainbow Falls. Named for the afternoon rainbows arching through its mist, it is an 80-foot waterfall that often freezes in an hourglass shape during winter months. Climb to an elevation

of 6,643 feet at Clingmans Dome, the highest peak in the Smoky Mountains. Hike the 11-mile loop around Cades Cove, and spend a day camping, horseback riding, or settling down for a picnic in this famous scenic valley. It is no surprise that Great Smoky Mountains National Park is the most visited national park in the country—with idyllic snowfall in the winter, explosions of wildflowers in the spring and summer, and classic autumn colors, you can never go wrong with a visit to this expansive park.

OCTOBER 2025

NOTES	SUNDAY	MONDAY	TUESDAY
		5	6 ●	7
		LABOUR DAY (AUS-ACT/NSW/SA)	SUKKOT (BEGINS AT SUNDOWN)
	12 ☾	13	14
		INDIGENOUS PEOPLES' DAY (US) COLUMBUS DAY (US) THANKSGIVING DAY (CAN)	
	19	20 ○	21
☽	26	27	28
		LABOUR DAY (NZ)	

OCTOBER 2025

WEDNESDAY	THURSDAY	FRIDAY	SATURDAY
1	2	3	4
	YOM KIPPUR (BEGINS AT SUNDOWN)		
8	9	10	11
15	16	17	18
SIMCHAT TORAH (BEGINS AT SUNDOWN)			
22	23	24	25
29	30	31	
		HALLOWEEN	

GREAT SMOKY MOUNTAINS NATIONAL PARK

LOCATION: North Carolina–Tennessee border

SIZE: 522,427 acres

BEST TIME TO VISIT: May through September

NATURE: This park is home to more than 1,400 species of flowering plants such as wild petunias, goldenrod, pinesap, snakeroot, sweet birch, and touch-me-nots, as well as more than 4,000 species of non-flowering plants.

HABITATS: The park boasts more than 400 species of vertebrates, including the northern flying squirrel, smoky madtom, Peregrine Falcon, and white-tailed deer—along with about 1,500 American black bears! It also has more than 9,000 species of insects.

ACTIVITIES: Auto touring, biking, camping, fishing, hiking, horseback riding, and picnicking.

NATURAL FEATURES: Alum Cave, Baskins Creek Falls, Cades Cove, Chimney Tops, Clingmans Dome (the highest point in Tennessee), Grotto Falls, and Newfound Gap.

SEPTEMBER/OCTOBER

MONDAY (SEPTEMBER) ◗   **29**

TUESDAY (SEPTEMBER)   **30**

WEDNESDAY   **1**

THURSDAY YOM KIPPUR (BEGINS AT SUNDOWN)   **2**

FRIDAY   **3**

SATURDAY   **4**

SUNDAY   **5**

OCTOBER 2025

MONDAY LABOUR DAY (AUS-ACT/NSW/SA) **6**

TUESDAY SUKKOT (BEGINS AT SUNDOWN) ● **7**

WEDNESDAY **8**

THURSDAY **9**

FRIDAY   **10**

SATURDAY   **11**

SUNDAY   **12**

Of the 2,900 miles of streams in the Smoky Mountains, it contains one of the last wild trout habitats in the United States.

OCTOBER 2025

MONDAY   INDIGENOUS PEOPLES' DAY (US) / COLUMBUS DAY (US) / THANKSGIVING DAY (CAN)   ◖   **13**

TUESDAY   **14**

WEDNESDAY   SIMCHAT TORAH (BEGINS AT SUNDOWN)   **15**

THURSDAY   **16**

FRIDAY

17

SATURDAY

18

SUNDAY

19

This park is also known as the Wildflower National Park. Partake in the Spring Wildflower Pilgrimage, an event that features professionally guided walks and exhibits of the region's rich nature.

OCTOBER 2025

MONDAY 20

TUESDAY ○ 21

WEDNESDAY 22

THURSDAY 23

FRIDAY 24

SATURDAY 25

SUNDAY 26

The Cherokee named this area "Land of Blue Smoke" because the fog, which is created by transpiration, tends to scatter blue light.

NOVEMBER
Saguaro National Park

Imagine a classic, cliché, cacti-filled desert—chances are, you are picturing Saguaro National Park. On either side of Tucson, Arizona, the Tucson Mountain District and Rincon Mountain District are home to the iconic, tree-sized saguaro cacti. These cartoonish cacti are only found in the Sonoran Desert, the hottest desert in both the US and Mexico. The park's archeological sites trace back to the Archaic period, and you can explore Signal Hill, a boulder-covered hill with petroglyphs carved into the rock. You might also hike to Wassen Peak for stunning views or drive on the Cactus Forest Drive loop, stopping at the Desert Ecology Trail or

Javelina Rocks Overlook on the way. In either district, whether trekking across cacti-covered desert ground or succulent-spotted mountain climbs, be sure to bring plenty of water. And keep a safe distance from the Sonoran Desert fauna— from roadrunners to horned lizards to kangaroo rats. However, keep your camera ready to capture many stills of unparalleled desert vistas in Saguaro National Park, especially as the day approaches evening when consistently gorgeous sunsets take over the sky. And to prove you know your national parks, the correct pronunciation of saguaro is *sa-waro*.

NOVEMBER 2025

NOTES	SUNDAY	MONDAY	TUESDAY
	2	3	4
			ELECTION DAY (US)
	9	10	11
			VETERANS DAY (US)
	16	17	18
	23	24	25
	30		

NOVEMBER 2025

WEDNESDAY	THURSDAY	FRIDAY	SATURDAY
			1
			ALL SAINTS' DAY
● 5	6	7	8
◗ 12	13	14	15
19 ○	20	21	22
26	27 ◗	28	29
	THANKSGIVING DAY (US)	NATIVE AMERICAN HERITAGE DAY (US)	

SAGUARO NATIONAL PARK

LOCATION: Southeastern Arizona, on opposite sides of Tucson

SIZE: 91,327 acres

BEST TIME TO VISIT: October through May

NATURE: Saguaro boasts more than 3,500 different plant species, such as alligator juniper, blue paloverde, ironwood, mountain mahogany, saguaro cacti, and velvet mesquite.

HABITATS: The park is home to more than 300 species of vertebrates, including the canyon treefrog, elf owl, Gila monster, javelina, and roadrunner.

ACTIVITIES: Auto touring, camping, hiking, picnicking, mountain biking, watching sunsets, and viewing ancient petroglyphs.

NATURAL FEATURES: Bridal Wreath Falls, Mica Mountain, Tanque Verde Ridge, Rincon Creek, Wasson Peak, and more!

MONDAY (OCTOBER) LABOUR DAY (NZ)

27

TUESDAY (OCTOBER)

28

WEDNESDAY (OCTOBER)

29

THURSDAY (OCTOBER)

30

FRIDAY (OCTOBER) HALLOWEEN

31

SATURDAY ALL SAINTS' DAY

1

SUNDAY

2

NOVEMBER 2025

MONDAY   **3**

TUESDAY ELECTION DAY (US)   **4**

WEDNESDAY ●   **5**

THURSDAY   **6**

FRIDAY

7

SATURDAY

8

SUNDAY

9

The park has a citizen science program called the Gila Monster Project, which collects photos of and information about this mysterious, venomous lizard.

NOVEMBER 2025

MONDAY **10**

TUESDAY VETERANS DAY (US) **11**

WEDNESDAY **12**

THURSDAY **13**

FRIDAY

14

SATURDAY

15

SUNDAY

16

Saguaro cacti do not grow their distinctive arms until around age 75.

NOVEMBER 2025

MONDAY 17

TUESDAY 18

WEDNESDAY 19

THURSDAY ○ 20

FRIDAY

21

SATURDAY

22

SUNDAY

23

Indigenous people have been eating Saguaro cacti fruit for centuries—it is bright red, tastes faintly like strawberry, and makes a great jam or syrup.

NOVEMBER 2025

MONDAY 24

TUESDAY 25

WEDNESDAY 26

THURSDAY THANKSGIVING DAY (US) 27

FRIDAY NATIVE AMERICAN HERITAGE DAY (US) ◗ **28**

SATURDAY **29**

SUNDAY **30**

In 1990, Saguaro National Park experienced its hottest recorded temperature, at a lethal 117 degrees Fahrenheit.

DECEMBER
Yellowstone National Park

Containing half of the world's hydrothermal features, from fumaroles to geysers to mud pots, Yellowstone National Park is an explosive natural wonderland. Established in 1872, Yellowstone National Park existed before Wyoming, Idaho, and Montana—the three states it sprawls across—were made official states. The park lies atop a super volcano; around two million years ago, an enormous volcanic eruption created the vast caldera in the center of the park. Smaller eruptions, steam explosions, and 1,000 to 3,000 annual earthquakes have been shaping the land since. Visit Old Faithful—a geyser named for the regularity of its eruptions—every

44 minutes to 2 hours. Drive down Grand Loop Road or hike into Hayden Valley to spot the world's largest rut of free-roaming bison. Explore the limestone terraces of Mammoth Hot Springs, but don't touch—this water can be boiling and somewhat acidic. The magic of the park is endless, from the 20-mile-long Yellowstone Lake to the brightly colored rainbow rings and cerulean center of the Grand Prismatic Spring. Yellowstone's temperature swings to both extremes, so dress appropriately for the season to let your curious inner scientist focus entirely on the more than 10,000 hydrothermal wonders around you.

DECEMBER 2025

NOTES	SUNDAY	MONDAY	TUESDAY
		1	2
		WORLD AIDS DAY	
	7	8	9
	14	15	16
	21	22	23
	WINTER SOLSTICE		
	28	29	30

DECEMBER 2025

WEDNESDAY	THURSDAY	FRIDAY	SATURDAY
3 ●	**4**	**5**	**6**
INTERNATIONAL DAY OF PERSONS WITH DISABILITIES			
10 ☽	**11**	**12**	**13**
HUMAN RIGHTS DAY			
17	**18**	**19** ○	**20**
24	**25**	**26** ☽	**27**
CHRISTMAS EVE	CHRISTMAS DAY HANUKKAH (BEGINS AT SUNDOWN)	BOXING DAY (UK/CAN/AUS/NZ) FIRST DAY OF KWANZAA	
31			
NEW YEAR'S EVE			

YELLOWSTONE NATIONAL PARK

LOCATION: Northwestern Wyoming spreading into Montana and Idaho

SIZE: 2,221,766 acres

BEST TIME TO VISIT: May through October

NATURE: Yellowstone boasts more than 1,300 species of flowering plants, such as fringed gentian, lodgepole pine, quaking aspens, paintbrush, and Rocky Mountain maple.

HABITATS: The park is home to almost 400 species of animals, including the bald eagle, bison, cutthroat trout, pronghorn, and gray wolf.

ACTIVITIES: Biking, boating, camping, fishing, hiking, horseback riding, swimming, and winter activities (skiing, snowshoeing, and snowmobiling).

NATURAL FEATURES: Artist Point, Hayden Valley, Mammoth Hot Springs, Mud Volcano, Norris Geyser Basin, Old Faithful (erupting around twenty times a day), Specimen Ridge, Steamboat Geyser (the world's tallest active geyser), and Yellowstone Lake and River.

DECEMBER

MONDAY WORLD AIDS DAY — **1**

TUESDAY — **2**

WEDNESDAY INTERNATIONAL DAY OF PERSONS WITH DISABILITIES — **3**

THURSDAY ● — **4**

FRIDAY — **5**

SATURDAY — **6**

SUNDAY — **7**

DECEMBER 2025

MONDAY 8

TUESDAY 9

WEDNESDAY HUMAN RIGHTS DAY 10

THURSDAY 11

FRIDAY 12

SATURDAY 13

SUNDAY 14

In 1870, Truman C. Everts got lost in Yellowstone for a harrowing 37 days, managing to subsist on a thistle plant that was later named Everts thistle.

DECEMBER 2025

MONDAY   **15**

TUESDAY   **16**

WEDNESDAY   **17**

THURSDAY   **18**

FRIDAY   **19**

SATURDAY ○   **20**

SUNDAY WINTER SOLSTICE   **21**

*Twenty-seven modern Native American tribes have
ancestry associated with Yellowstone, due to its many
natural resources and location at the intersection of the
Great Basin, Great Plains, and Columbia Plateau.*

DECEMBER 2025

MONDAY   22

TUESDAY   23

WEDNESDAY CHRISTMAS EVE   24

THURSDAY CHRISTMAS DAY / HANUKKAH (BEGINS AT SUNDOWN)   25

FRIDAY BOXING DAY (UK/CAN/AUS/NZ) / FIRST DAY OF KWANZAA **26**

SATURDAY ☽ **27**

SUNDAY **28**

From 1890 to the Second World War, Yellowstone's visitors enjoyed nightly bear shows, in which black and grizzly bears would eat from the park's garbage heap.

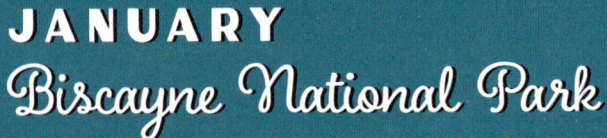

JANUARY
Biscayne National Park

Located in the northern Florida Keys, Biscayne National Park is an aquatic safe haven for endangered manatees, various sea turtles, and more than 600 native species of fish. Hear the squawking seabirds and feel the salty spray of aquamarine water as you boat by mangrove forests and the world's third largest barrier reef. Biscayne National Park, established in 1980, is 95 percent underwater—so although you can hike the scenic Jetty Trail, the true Biscayne experience begins when you step off the land. Snorkel through the history of Biscayne Bay with the Maritime Heritage Trail, leading to six shipwrecks and Fowey Rocks Lighthouse,

also known as the Eye of Miami. Evidence of 10,000 years of human history has been dredged up from the bottom of the bay, from prehistoric tribes to pineapple farmers. There are more than 50 shipwrecks preserved in the park; these wrecks were due to a combination of shallow shores, hurricanes, coastal reefs, and pirates. Yes, pirates. The exterior waters of the park were once a superhighway for pirates and privateers. But Biscayne National Park ensures that modern pirates do not pillage any shipwrecks, so don't worry about encountering them as you dive into the fish-bejeweled coral.

JANUARY 2026

NOTES	SUNDAY	MONDAY	TUESDAY
		4	5	6
	11	12	13
○ 18	19	20
25 ☽	26	27

CIVIL RIGHTS DAY (US)

MARTIN LUTHER
KING JR. DAY (US)

AUSTRALIA DAY (AUS)

HOLOCAUST
REMEMBRANCE DAY

JANUARY 2026

WEDNESDAY	THURSDAY	FRIDAY	SATURDAY
	1	2 ●	3
	NEW YEAR'S DAY	NEW YEAR HOLIDAY (UK-SCT)	
7	8	9 ☽	10
14	15	16	17
21	22	23	24
28	29	30	31

BISCAYNE NATIONAL PARK

LOCATION: Southern Florida, approximately 1 hour south of Miami

SIZE: 172,971 acres

BEST TIME TO VISIT: November through April

NATURE: Biscayne boasts more than 350 different plant species, such as buccaneer palm, mangroves, paradise tree, seagrape, and semaphore cacti. Biscayne is also home to plenty of algae, such as turtle grass, manatee grass, and shoal grass.

HABITATS: The park is home to more than 800 species of vertebrates (600 of which are native species of fish), including the brown pelican, manatee, osprey, sea turtle, and snowy egret.

ACTIVITIES: Boating, camping, canoeing, diving, fishing, hiking, kayaking, lobstering, and snorkeling.

NATURAL FEATURES: Boca Chita Key, Caesar Creek, Elliot Key, Florida's Coral Reef, Jones Lagoon, and more!

DECEMBER/JANUARY

MONDAY (DECEMBER)   **29**

TUESDAY (DECEMBER)   **30**

WEDNESDAY (DECEMBER) NEW YEAR'S EVE   **31**

THURSDAY NEW YEAR'S DAY   **1**

FRIDAY NEW YEAR HOLIDAY (UK-SCT)   **2**

SATURDAY ●   **3**

SUNDAY   **4**

JANUARY 2026

MONDAY 5

TUESDAY 6

WEDNESDAY 7

THURSDAY 8

FRIDAY 9

SATURDAY 🌓 10

SUNDAY 11

Biscayne served as the headquarters for Black Caesar, a notorious African pirate who roamed the Caribbean in the 1700s.

JANUARY 2026

MONDAY **12**

TUESDAY **13**

WEDNESDAY **14**

THURSDAY **15**

FRIDAY 16

SATURDAY 17

SUNDAY ○ 18

In the 1960s, the Central Intelligence Agency used Elliot Key as a training field to prepare for the Bay of Pigs Invasion in Cuba.

JANUARY 2026

MONDAY CIVIL RIGHTS DAY (US) / MARTIN LUTHER KING JR. DAY (US) **19**

TUESDAY **20**

WEDNESDAY **21**

THURSDAY **22**

FRIDAY   **23**

SATURDAY   **24**

SUNDAY   **25**

Biscayne Bay has an average depth of 10 feet, making it an incredibly shallow sea.

FEBRUARY
Grand Canyon National Park

As one of the Seven Wonders of the World, the Grand Canyon is a mysterious national park to be both marveled at and humbled by. The park, established in 1919, is a vast, legendary landscape with distinctive North, South, and West Rims. The canyon is made up of stunning layers of sedimentary rock—dating back to the Precambrian period—and distinctive cliffs of pink, red, and orange. Find some of the best views after a 2.2-mile trek from Shoshone Point or to the most remote viewpoint from Toroweap Overlook, where 3,000 feet below flows the largest

rapid in the Colorado River. If you plan to go out and see it all in person, grab a few friends and bring plenty of water because the inner canyon will be sweltering. When you are well prepared, visiting the iconic Grand Canyon can be the experience of a lifetime. Stand 4,000 feet over the canyon on the gravity-defying Skywalk at the West Rim or take a mule ride over to Phantom Ranch or down to Kaibab National Forest. And don't miss Desert View Drive, a jaw-dropping 25-mile tour along the Colorado River, the dynamic body of water that carved this national treasure.

FEBRUARY 2026

NOTES	SUNDAY	MONDAY	TUESDAY
	● 1	2	3
	FIRST DAY OF BLACK HISTORY MONTH	GROUNDHOG DAY (US/CAN)	
	8 ◑	9	10
	15	16 ○	17
		PRESIDENTS' DAY (US)	CHINESE NEW YEAR RAMADAN (BEGINS AT SUNDOWN)
	22	23 ◗	24

FEBRUARY 2026

WEDNESDAY	THURSDAY	FRIDAY	SATURDAY
4	5	6	7
		WAITANGI DAY OBSERVED (NZ)	
11	12	13	14
			VALENTINE'S DAY
18	19	20	21
ASH WEDNESDAY			
25	26	27	28

GRAND CANYON NATIONAL PARK

LOCATION: Northwestern Arizona

SIZE: 1,218,375 acres

BEST TIME TO VISIT: April through June

NATURE: Grand Canyon National Park is home to approximately 1,700 vascular plants such as coyote willow, catclaw acacia, Utah juniper, ponderosa pine, quaking aspen, and cliffrose.

HABITATS: The park boasts approximately 600 species of vertebrates including the chuckwalla lizard, mule deer, desert bighorn sheep, and striped whipsnake.

ACTIVITIES: Biking, camping, helicopter touring, hiking, mule riding, river rafting, and sightseeing.

NATURAL FEATURES: Colorado River, Deer Creek Falls, Elves Chasm, Hermit Trail and Rapid, Pearce Ferry, Tapeats Creek, Uinkaret volcanic field, and more!

JANUARY/FEBRUARY

MONDAY (JANUARY) AUSTRALIA DAY (AUS) ◗ **26**

TUESDAY (JANUARY) HOLOCAUST REMEMBRANCE DAY **27**

WEDNESDAY (JANUARY) **28**

THURSDAY (JANUARY) **29**

FRIDAY (JANUARY) **30**

SATURDAY (JANUARY) **31**

SUNDAY FIRST DAY OF BLACK HISTORY MONTH ● **1**

FEBRUARY 2026

MONDAY GROUNDHOG DAY (US/CAN)   **2**

TUESDAY   **3**

WEDNESDAY   **4**

THURSDAY   **5**

FRIDAY WAITANGI DAY OBSERVED (NZ) 6

SATURDAY 7

SUNDAY 8

Grand Canyon National Park has the most frequent human disappearances of all the national parks, at well over 1,000 since its founding.

FEBRUARY 2026

MONDAY ◖   **9**

TUESDAY   **10**

WEDNESDAY   **11**

THURSDAY   **12**

FRIDAY   **13**

SATURDAY VALENTINE'S DAY   **14**

SUNDAY   **15**

Supai Village, the most remote community in the lower 48 states, is located within the canyon. It has a population of 208.

FEBRUARY 2026

MONDAY PRESIDENTS' DAY (US)

16

TUESDAY CHINESE NEW YEAR / RAMADAN (BEGINS AT SUNDOWN) ○

17

WEDNESDAY ASH WEDNESDAY

18

THURSDAY

19

FRIDAY 20

SATURDAY 21

SUNDAY 22

On average, 250 people must be rescued from inside the Grand Canyon every year—so always be careful and prepared for your hikes!

MARCH
Great Basin National Park

In the Great Basin Desert, no runoff reaches the ocean. Instead, the stunningly clear glacial streams and creeks empty into the lakes we cherish at Great Basin National Park. Although many hear the word *desert* and picture dry, barren land, the Great Basin is rich with wildlife and awe-inspiring mountains, protecting a chunk of Nevada's famed Snake Range. The park, established in 1986, has evidence of thousands of years of archeological history, from the sedentary Fremont peoples to South Snake Range mining camps. Great Basin is an International Dark Sky Park, so spend a clear night camping under the Andromeda Galaxy, gazing up at

Jupiter, Mars, and Saturn. During the day, tour the Lehman Caves, a honeycomb of tunnels filled with white limestone stalactites and stalagmites. Visit the scraggly, breathtaking Ancient Bristlecone Pine Forest, home to some of the oldest trees in the world. Climb the 6-story limestone Lexington Arch or one of the windiest, rockiest, steepest hikes, the Wheeler Peak Summit. Once you make it to the top, the site is home to Nevada's only glacier, at 11,500 feet in elevation. On a clear day, witness the most incredible view of more than 100 miles of the Wheeler and Doso Doyabi mountains.

MARCH 2026

NOTES	SUNDAY	MONDAY	TUESDAY
	1	**2**	● **3**
	FIRST DAY OF WOMEN'S HISTORY MONTH		PURIM (BEGINS AT SUNDOWN)
	8	**9**	**10**
		LABOUR DAY (AUS-VIC)	
	15	**16**	**17**
	MOTHERING SUNDAY (UK)		ST. PATRICK'S DAY
	22	**23**	**24**
	29	**30**	**31**
	PALM SUNDAY		

MARCH 2026

WEDNESDAY	THURSDAY	FRIDAY	SATURDAY
4	5	6	7
◖ 11	12	13	14
18 ○	19	20	21
◗ 25	26 EID AL-FITR (BEGINS AT SUNSET)	27 SPRING EQUINOX NOWRUZ	28

GREAT BASIN NATIONAL PARK

LOCATION: Eastern Nevada

SIZE: 77,180 acres

BEST TIME TO VISIT: April through October

NATURE: This park boasts more than 800 different plant species, such as blue elderberry, bristlecone pine, Engelmann spruce, sagebrush, wild rose, and white fir.

HABITATS: The park is home to more than 300 species of vertebrates, including the beaver, mountain lion, porcupine, pygmy rabbit, water shrew, and yellow-bellied marmot.

ACTIVITIES: Auto touring, biking, camping, cave touring, fishing, hiking, picnicking, pine nut gathering, and stargazing.

NATURAL FEATURES: Alpine Lakes, Ancient Bristlecone Pine Forest, Crystal Peak, Lehman Caves, Lexington Arch, Stella Lake, and Wheeler Peak.

FEBRUARY/MARCH

MONDAY (FEBRUARY)   **23**

TUESDAY (FEBRUARY) ◗   **24**

WEDNESDAY (FEBRUARY)   **25**

THURSDAY (FEBRUARY)   **26**

FRIDAY (FEBRUARY)   **27**

SATURDAY (FEBRUARY)   **28**

SUNDAY   FIRST DAY OF WOMEN'S HISTORY MONTH   **1**

MARCH 2026

MONDAY 2

TUESDAY PURIM (BEGINS AT SUNDOWN) ● 3

WEDNESDAY 4

THURSDAY 5

FRIDAY 6

SATURDAY 7

SUNDAY 8

Attend the Great Basin Astronomy Festival in September and explore one of the deepest, darkest night skies in the country!

MARCH 2026

MONDAY   **9**

TUESDAY   **10**

WEDNESDAY ☾   **11**

THURSDAY   **12**

FRIDAY 13

SATURDAY 14

SUNDAY MOTHERING SUNDAY (UK) 15

The Bonneville cutthroat trout is Great Basin National Park's very own native fish species, found in cold streams and at very high altitudes.

MARCH 2026

MONDAY   **16**

TUESDAY ST. PATRICK'S DAY   **17**

WEDNESDAY   **18**

THURSDAY EID AL-FITR (BEGINS AT SUNSET) ○   **19**

FRIDAY SPRING EQUINOX / NOWRUZ

20

SATURDAY

21

SUNDAY

22

An ancient bristlecone tree lived for almost 5,000 years in the park before being cut down for research—it was named Prometheus, after the Titan god who gave humans fire.

MARCH 2026

MONDAY 23

TUESDAY 24

WEDNESDAY ☽ 25

THURSDAY 26

FRIDAY 27

SATURDAY 28

SUNDAY PALM SUNDAY 29

A pictograph is a rock painting, and a petroglyph is a rock carving. The Fremont people left behind both art forms in the Great Basin around 1000 to 1300 CE.

APRIL
Yosemite National Park

Tucked in the heart of California's Sierra Nevada mountains, Yosemite boasts a majestic combination of cascading waterfalls, sprawling meadows, granite cliffs, twinkling streams, and giant sequoia groves. The park, established in 1890, was first officially protected by Abraham Lincoln in 1864 under the Yosemite Valley Grant Act. And there is no question why—Yosemite National Park is an idyllic slice of the most magnificent nature America has to offer. Gaze through the rays of a moonbow—created by the rays of the moon instead of the sun—bouncing off Yosemite Falls, one of the tallest waterfalls in the world at 1,430 feet. In the

Tuolumne or Mariposa Grove of Giant Sequoias, come face to face with the largest form of life on our planet—and even duck through gaps in their trunks. Rock-climb in the very birthplace of the sport, digging into the granite cracks of the Merced River Canyon or the domes of Tuolumne Meadows. Hike the iconic El Capitan, reaching an elevation of 7,573 feet, or conquer one of Yosemite's hardest hikes with Half Dome, which requires metal cables to climb the last 400 feet. On your adventures, spot roaming wildlife such as black bears and mule deer, but especially keep an eye out for the highly endangered, extremely elusive Sierra Nevada red fox.

APRIL 2026

NOTES	SUNDAY	MONDAY	TUESDAY
	5	**6**	**7**
	EASTER **12**	**13**	**14**
	ORTHODOX EASTER **19**	YOM HASHOAH (BEGINS AT SUNDOWN) **20**	**21**
	26	**27**	**28**

APRIL 2026

WEDNESDAY	THURSDAY	FRIDAY	SATURDAY
1 ●	2	3	4
APRIL FOOLS' DAY PASSOVER (BEGINS AT SUNDOWN)		GOOD FRIDAY	
8	9 ☾	10	11
15	16 ○	17	18
22	23 ☽	24	25
ADMINISTRATIVE PROFESSIONALS' DAY (US) EARTH DAY		ANZAC DAY (AUS/NZ)	
29	30		

YOSEMITE NATIONAL PARK

LOCATION: Central California, approximately 3.5 hours SE of Sacramento

SIZE: 748,542 acres

BEST TIME TO VISIT: May through October

NATURE: Yosemite is home to almost 1,400 vascular plant species, such as California black oak, giant sequoia, marsh marigold, mountain hemlock, red fir, and scarlet monkeyflower.

HABITATS: The park boasts more than 400 species of vertebrates, including the American pika, black bear, California mountain kingsnake, Steller's jay, wild boar, and yellow-bellied marmot.

ACTIVITIES: Auto touring, biking, birdwatching, boating, camping, fishing, hiking, horseback riding, photography, rafting, rock climbing, stargazing, swimming, and winter activities.

NATURAL FEATURES: Bridalveil Fall, Clouds Rest, El Capitan, Emerald Pool, Glacier Point, Half Dome, Tenaya Lake, Yosemite Falls, and more!

MARCH/APRIL

MONDAY (MARCH)   **30**

TUESDAY (MARCH)   **31**

WEDNESDAY APRIL FOOLS' DAY / PASSOVER (BEGINS AT SUNDOWN)   **1**

THURSDAY ●   **2**

FRIDAY GOOD FRIDAY   **3**

SATURDAY   **4**

SUNDAY EASTER   **5**

APRIL 2026

MONDAY **6**

TUESDAY **7**

WEDNESDAY **8**

THURSDAY **9**

FRIDAY ☽ **10**

SATURDAY **11**

SUNDAY ORTHODOX EASTER **12**

The Ahwahnee Hotel, Yosemite's most popular hotel, was once used as a Second World War naval hospital.

APRIL 2026

MONDAY YOM HASHOAH (BEGINS AT SUNDOWN)   **13**

TUESDAY   **14**

WEDNESDAY   **15**

THURSDAY   **16**

FRIDAY ○ **17**

SATURDAY **18**

SUNDAY **19**

The Sierra Nevada mountains in Yosemite are actively growing at a rate of 1 foot every 1,000 years.

APRIL 2026

MONDAY   **20**

TUESDAY   **21**

WEDNESDAY ADMINISTRATIVE PROFESSIONALS' DAY (US) / EARTH DAY   **22**

THURSDAY   **23**

FRIDAY ◗ **24**

SATURDAY ANZAC DAY (AUS/NZ) **25**

SUNDAY **26**

Yosemite is home to 3 of the 10 highest waterfalls in the world.

MAY
Badlands National Park

It might be called Badlands, but this park is anything but bad. Filled with sharply eroded rock formations and surrounded by sprawling grasslands, Badlands National Park is otherworldly in its landscape. About 75 million years ago, deposition of rocks and sediments formed Pierre Shale, the park's geologic base. After almost fifty million years of deposition, the rocks were fully formed in height, ready for erosion to grip the landscape. The Cheyenne and White Rivers carved narrow channels and canyons through the Badlands, leaving behind a geologic marvel that is home to elk, pronghorn, deer, mountain lions, and dozens of bird species. Visit

the Fossil Preparation Lab to learn about the more than 13,000 bones that have been excavated from the park for research and the mustard-colored hills made of fossilized soils. Hike the Notch Trail by climbing up a wooden ladder, walking along cliff edges, and exploring stunning canyons. Drive the 30-mile Badlands Loop Road, stopping at Panorama Point or the Yellow Mounds Overlook for a breathtaking sunset. If you become a huge fan of this park, plan an excursion every couple of years, because this geologic masterpiece is a work in progress that is constantly changing.

MAY 2026

NOTES	SUNDAY	MONDAY	TUESDAY
		3	**4**	**5**
		LABOUR DAY (AUS-QLD) EARLY MAY BANK HOLIDAY (UK)	CINCO DE MAYO
	10	**11**	**12**
	MOTHER'S DAY (US/CAN)		
	17	**18**	**19**
		VICTORIA DAY (CAN)	
	24	**25**	**26**
	● **31**	SPRING BANK HOLIDAY (UK) MEMORIAL DAY (US)	

MAY 2026

WEDNESDAY	THURSDAY	FRIDAY	SATURDAY
		● 1	2
		FIRST DAY OF ASIAN AMERICAN AND PACIFIC ISLANDER HERITAGE MONTH	
6	7	8 ☾	9
13	14	15 ○	16
20	21	22 ☽	23
27	28	29	30

BADLANDS NATIONAL PARK

LOCATION: Southwestern South Dakota, approximately 4 hours west of Sioux Falls

SIZE: 242,756 acres

BEST TIME TO VISIT: April through November

NATURE: The park is home to more than 400 different plant species, such as Rocky Mountain juniper, spiny phlox, sagebrush, western wheatgrass, wooly verbena, and yellow sweet clover.

HABITATS: Badlands boasts more than 250 species of vertebrates, including the bison, prairie dog, pronghorn, sharp-tailed grouse, and white-tailed deer.

ACTIVITIES: Auto touring, biking, camping, hiking, horseback riding, sunset and sunrise watching, and stargazing.

NATURAL FEATURES: Badlands Wall, Roberts Prairie Dog Town, Sage Creek, White River Valley, and the Yellow Mounds.

APRIL/MAY

MONDAY (APRIL) — **27**

TUESDAY (APRIL) — **28**

WEDNESDAY (APRIL) — **29**

THURSDAY (APRIL) — **30**

FRIDAY — FIRST DAY OF ASIAN AMERICAN AND PACIFIC ISLANDER HERITAGE MONTH ● — **1**

SATURDAY — **2**

SUNDAY — **3**

MAY 2026

MONDAY LABOUR DAY (AUS-QLD) / EARLY MAY BANK HOLIDAY (UK) 4

TUESDAY CINCO DE MAYO 5

WEDNESDAY 6

THURSDAY 7

FRIDAY   **8**

SATURDAY   **9**

SUNDAY MOTHER'S DAY (US/CAN)   **10**

Badlands was named by the Lakota people, who called it "mako sica," which means "land that is bad," due to its lack of water and difficult-to-traverse topography.

MAY 2026

MONDAY 11

TUESDAY 12

WEDNESDAY 13

THURSDAY 14

FRIDAY   **15**

SATURDAY ○   **16**

SUNDAY   **17**

80 to 75 million years ago, Badlands National Park was an inland sea known as the Western Interior Seaway.

MAY 2026

MONDAY VICTORIA DAY (CAN)　　　　　　　　　　　**18**

TUESDAY　　　　　　　　　　　**19**

WEDNESDAY　　　　　　　　　　　**20**

THURSDAY　　　　　　　　　　　**21**

FRIDAY

22

SATURDAY ◗

23

SUNDAY

24

The park's Pine Ridge Reservation was seized by the Department of the Army during the Second World War to be used as a practice bombing range.

MAY 2026

MONDAY SPRING BANK HOLIDAY (UK) / MEMORIAL DAY (US)   **25**

TUESDAY   **26**

WEDNESDAY   **27**

THURSDAY   **28**

FRIDAY 29

SATURDAY 30

SUNDAY ● 31

Due to its otherworldly terrain, the park has been the setting for alien planets and asteroid landings in blockbuster hits such as STARSHIP TROOPERS (1997) and ARMAGEDDON (1998).

JUNE
Acadia National Park

Named after the Grecian Arcadia for its classic rugged shoreline, Acadia National Park is a rocky Atlantic sanctuary on the midsection of Maine's coast. The park, established in 1919, is bursting with wildlife and breathtaking sights, but also with history. Acadia's archeological evidence dates back more than 10,000 years to the Wabanaki people. More recently, a 1947 fire decimated 10,000 acres of the park, engulfing spruce and fir trees alike. Although birch and aspen grew in their place, the park is still working spruce and fir back into its ecology. For a quick

but comprehensive tour of Acadia, take the 27-mile Park Loop Road, stopping at Sand Beach, Precipice Trail, and Otter Cliff along the way. Hear the thunderous echoes at Thunder Hole, a cave with an impressive spray zone of up to 40 feet. Ride a horse down the Carriage Road system, explore the craggy shoreline of the secluded Schoodic Peninsula, or climb Cadillac Mountain, the tallest mountain on the eastern seaboard at 1,530 feet. Acadia is charming no matter the season—from winter snow sports to vibrant fall colors to beautiful summer weather.

JUNE 2026

NOTES	SUNDAY	MONDAY	TUESDAY
		1	**2**
		FIRST DAY OF PRIDE MONTH	
	7 ☽	**8**	**9**
	14 ○	**15**	**16**
	FLAG DAY (US)		
☽ **21**	**22**	**23**
	FATHER'S DAY (US/CAN/UK) SUMMER SOLSTICE		
	28 ●	**29**	**30**

JUNE 2026

WEDNESDAY	THURSDAY	FRIDAY	SATURDAY
3	4	5	6
10	11	12	13
17	18	19 JUNETEENTH (US)	20
24	25	26	27

ACADIA NATIONAL PARK

LOCATION: Eastern Maine

SIZE: 49,075 acres

BEST TIME TO VISIT: June through October

NATURE: Acadia boasts more than 1,100 different plant species, such as bunchberry, black crowberry, cinnamon fern, goldenrod, northern white cedar, and wild lily-of-the-valley.

HABITATS: The park is home to more than 400 species of vertebrates, including the brown bat, beaver, mink, pickerel frog, snowshoe hare, spotted salamander, and white-tailed deer.

ACTIVITIES: Biking, birdwatching, boating, diving, exploring tide pools, fishing, hiking, stargazing, and swimming.

NATURAL FEATURES: Bubble Rock, Cadillac Mountain, Echo Lake, Jordan Pond, Otter Cliff, Schoodic Peninsula, Thunder Hole, and more!

JUNE

MONDAY FIRST DAY OF PRIDE MONTH 1

TUESDAY 2

WEDNESDAY 3

THURSDAY 4

FRIDAY 5

SATURDAY 6

SUNDAY 7

JUNE 2026

MONDAY ☽   **8**

TUESDAY   **9**

WEDNESDAY   **10**

THURSDAY   **11**

FRIDAY   **12**

SATURDAY   **13**

SUNDAY   FLAG DAY (US)   **14**

*If you visit Cadillac Mountain between October and
March, you will be one of the first people in the country
to see the sun rise.*

JUNE 2026

MONDAY ○   **15**

TUESDAY   **16**

WEDNESDAY   **17**

THURSDAY   **18**

FRIDAY JUNETEENTH (US)

19

SATURDAY

20

SUNDAY FATHER'S DAY (US/CAN/UK) / SUMMER SOLSTICE ◗

21

Acadia is one of the bottom 10 national parks by size, but one of the top 10 by number of visitors.

JUNE 2026

MONDAY   **22**

TUESDAY   **23**

WEDNESDAY   **24**

THURSDAY   **25**

FRIDAY   **26**

SATURDAY   **27**

SUNDAY   **28**

John D. Rockefeller Jr. funded 45 miles of intricate carriage roads throughout the park. Its guardrail granite stones are affectionately called Rockefeller's teeth.

JULY
Guadalupe Mountains National Park

We are lucky to be alive at a time when this west Texan national treasure is no longer an underwater world at the bottom of the sea, but instead, something we can breathe in and trek through. What was once the Permian Basin's Delaware Sea has, over the past 260 million years, evaporated to reveal the staggering Guadalupe Mountains. The park contains the fossiliferous limestone of an enormous ancient coral reef near the New Mexico border. Established in 1972, Guadalupe Mountains National Park is also home to Texas's 4 highest peaks—Bush Mountain, Shumard, Bartlett Peaks, and Guadalupe—all curving around the Chihuahuan Desert's

iconic Pine Spring Canyon. Hike to an elevation of 8,751 feet at Guadalupe Peak, affectionately known as the Top of Texas. Trek through the sunbaked Salt Basin Dunes, which are made up of gypsum grains and scattered with vegetation. Visit the Frijole Ranch History Museum to get into the spirit of the American West, or explore the brilliant foliage and black-tailed rattlesnakes in McKittrick Canyon. As one of the nation's least visited parks, the remote nature of Guadalupe Mountains National Park makes it the perfect place to escape from the noise and chaos of the world.

JULY 2026

NOTES	SUNDAY	MONDAY	TUESDAY
	5	6 ◐	7
	12	13 ○	14
	19	20 ☽	21
	26	27	28

JULY 2026

WEDNESDAY	THURSDAY	FRIDAY	SATURDAY
1	2	3	4
CANADA DAY (CAN)			INDEPENDENCE DAY (US)
8	9	10	11
15	16	17	18
22	23	24	25
● 29	30	31	

GUADALUPE MOUNTAINS
NATIONAL PARK

LOCATION: Western Texas, approximately 2 hours east of El Paso

SIZE: 86,367 acres

BEST TIME TO VISIT: March through November

NATURE: This park is home to more than 1,000 species of plants, such as Apache plume, catclaw acacia, desert buckthorn, mistletoe, prickly pear cactus, and soaptree yucca.

HABITATS: The park boasts more than 400 species of vertebrates, including the badger, black-tailed jackrabbit, kit fox, long-eared sunfish, and mountain patchnose snake.

ACTIVITIES: Auto touring, backpacking, camping, hiking, horseback riding, and sunrise/sunset watching.

NATURAL FEATURES: Devil's Hall, Dog Canyon, Guadalupe Peak, Hunter Peak, McKittrick Canyon, Salt Basin Dunes, and the Grotto.

JUNE/JULY

MONDAY (JUNE) ● — 29

TUESDAY (JUNE) — 30

WEDNESDAY CANADA DAY (CAN) — 1

THURSDAY — 2

FRIDAY — 3

SATURDAY INDEPENDENCE DAY (US) — 4

SUNDAY — 5

JULY 2026

MONDAY 6

TUESDAY ☾ 7

WEDNESDAY 8

THURSDAY 9

FRIDAY　　　　　　　　　　　　　**10**

SATURDAY　　　　　　　　　　　**11**

SUNDAY　　　　　　　　　　　　**12**

You will not find many scenic drives in Guadalupe Mountains National Park, so lace up those hiking boots to see the best sights by trail.

MONDAY 13

TUESDAY ◯ 14

WEDNESDAY 15

THURSDAY 16

FRIDAY 17

SATURDAY 18

SUNDAY 19

Guadalupe Mountains National Park is the site of the Captain Reef, the largest exposed fossil reef on earth.

JULY 2026

MONDAY   **20**

TUESDAY ☽   **21**

WEDNESDAY   **22**

THURSDAY   **23**

FRIDAY 24

SATURDAY 25

SUNDAY 26

On particularly clear nights in the park, stargazers can see the Milky Way and more than 11,000 stars.

AUGUST
Grand Teton National Park

Although Grand Teton is only 10 miles from Yellowstone, this mountainous park should not be a mere stop along the way but a destination of its own. Around 10 million years ago, shifting of the Teton fault resulted in a series of earthquakes, erecting the stunning Teton Range of the Rockies. These mountains make up Grand Teton's iconic, snowcapped skyline—every photographer's dream. From the pristine Jenny Lake to the mirror-like Oxbow Bend, Grand Teton is packed with spectacular sights that can be seen 24 hours a day, 365 days a year. If you're seeking a thrill,

whitewater raft on the winding Snake River or waterski on Jackson Lake. If you like hunting, the world's largest elk herd is in Grand Teton, migrating between the park and the nearby National Elk Refuge. Grab your gear and join the annual elk reduction program. Drive up the sides of the mountain or hike the lush trail to Hidden Falls and Inspiration Point and take in a sprawling view of Jenny Lake. This is the only US national park with a commercial airport—the Jackson Hole Airport—so there's nothing stopping you from flying straight into this corner of Rocky Mountain heaven!

AUGUST 2026

NOTES	SUNDAY	MONDAY	TUESDAY
	2	3	4
		SUMMER BANK HOLIDAY (UK-SCT)	
	9	10	11
	16	17	18
	23	24	25
		SUMMER BANK HOLIDAY (UK-ENG/NIR/WAL)	
	30	31	

AUGUST 2026

WEDNESDAY	THURSDAY	FRIDAY	SATURDAY
			1
5 ☾	6	7	8
○ 12	13	14	15
19 ☽	20	21	22
26	27 ●	28	29

GRAND TETON NATIONAL PARK

LOCATION: Northwestern Wyoming

SIZE: 310,044 acres

BEST TIME TO VISIT: May through October

NATURE: Grand Teton boasts more than 1,000 species of vascular plants, such as blue spruce, calypso orchid, moss campion, rabbitbrush, sagebrush, sky pilot, and subalpine fir.

HABITATS: The park is home to more than 350 species of vertebrates, including the badger, black bear, grizzly bear, calliope hummingbird, mountain lion, Snake River spotted cutthroat trout, and trumpeter swan.

ACTIVITIES: Auto touring, biking, boating, camping, fishing, hiking, mountain climbing, photography, and winter activities.

NATURAL FEATURES: Colter Bay, Hidden Falls, Jenny Lake, Jackson Lake, Oxbow Bend, Signal Mountain, Snake River, and more!

MONDAY (JULY) 27

TUESDAY (JULY) 28

WEDNESDAY (JULY) ● 29

THURSDAY (JULY) 30

FRIDAY (JULY) 31

SATURDAY 1

SUNDAY 2

AUGUST 2026

MONDAY SUMMER BANK HOLIDAY (UK-SCT)

3

TUESDAY

4

WEDNESDAY

5

THURSDAY

6

FRIDAY 7

SATURDAY 8

SUNDAY 9

Hollywood star Wallace Berry led 500 head of cattle across Grand Teton National Park in a protest against the creation of the current park's boundaries.

MONDAY 10

TUESDAY 11

WEDNESDAY ○ 12

THURSDAY 13

FRIDAY 14

SATURDAY 15

SUNDAY 16

Grand Teton's beaver population might have been entirely destroyed had the fashion norm not shifted from fur hats to silk hats in the early 1800s.

AUGUST 2026

MONDAY   **17**

TUESDAY   **18**

WEDNESDAY   **19**

THURSDAY ◗   **20**

FRIDAY 21

SATURDAY 22

SUNDAY 23

Don't try to touch or disturb hibernating bears in the park—they are actually in a deep sleep called torpor, which they can wake up from!

AUGUST 2026

MONDAY SUMMER BANK HOLIDAY (UK-ENG/NIR/WAL) **24**

TUESDAY **25**

WEDNESDAY **26**

THURSDAY **27**

FRIDAY ●   **28**

SATURDAY   **29**

SUNDAY   **30**

Although Grand Teton's Jackson and Jenny Lakes have sparkling, crystal clear water, don't drink from them unless you want to risk catching a waterborne parasite.

SEPTEMBER
North Cascades National Park

Called the American Alps because of its snow-covered peaks, North Cascades National Park is one of the least visited and most remote US national parks. Although Highway 20 (North Cascades Scenic Highway) cuts through 120 miles of the land, large portions of the park's sprawling landscape are quite hard to access. But this Pacific Northwest gem is absolutely worth the extra navigation. With more than 500 sparkling lakes and ponds as well as a bounty of glaciers and snowcapped peaks, North Cascades provides breathtaking scenery and excellent conditions for plant growth. Over several thousand years, the North Cascades have been

home to Native Americans, miners, loggers, climbers, dam workers, and more. The first European known to explore this northern Washington mountain range was Alexander Ross, a Scottish employee looking for a trade route for the Pacific Fur Company. Now the park is famed for its opaque, turquoise Diablo Lake and its many gorgeous hiking trails. Take a short hike on the Newhalem Area Trails or a longer 4,040-foot-elevation hike to Monogram Lake, a dark blue pool filled with small, darting fish, surrounded by a mountainside blanketed in green. The North Cascades National Park is sure to grant you a peaceful trip whenever you visit.

SEPTEMBER 2026

NOTES	SUNDAY	MONDAY	TUESDAY
			1
	6	**7**	**8**
	FATHER'S DAY (AUS/NZ)	LABOR DAY (US) LABOUR DAY (CAN)	
	13	**14**	**15**
	GRANDPARENTS' DAY (US)		FIRST DAY OF NATIONAL HISPANIC HERITAGE MONTH
	20	**21**	**22**
	YOM KIPPUR (BEGINS AT SUNSET)		FALL EQUINOX
	27	**28**	**29**

SEPTEMBER 2026

WEDNESDAY	THURSDAY	FRIDAY	SATURDAY
2	3 ◐	4	5
9	10 ○	11	12
		PATRIOT DAY (US)	
16	17 ◑	18	19
23	24	25 ●	26
30			

NORTH CASCADES NATIONAL PARK

LOCATION: Northern Washington, approximately 2 hours NE of Seattle

SIZE: 504,781 acres

BEST TIME TO VISIT: May through October

NATURE: North Cascades boasts more than 1,600 vascular plant species, such as bracken ferns, foxglove, mountain thistle, Pacific silver fir, red columbine, and western red cedar.

HABITATS: The park is home to more than 300 species of vertebrates, including grizzly bears, wolverines, and rainbow trout, and more than 750 species of invertebrates, including the dreamy duskywing and woodland skipper.

ACTIVITIES: Biking, boating, camping, fishing, hiking, horseback riding, mountaineering, and winter activities.

NATURAL FEATURES: Cascade Pass, Colonial Creek Falls, Diablo Lake, Eldorado Peak, Hidden Lake, Forbidden Peak (a glacial horn!), Sahale Glacier, and Thornton Lakes.

AUGUST/SEPTEMBER

MONDAY (AUGUST) 31

TUESDAY 1

WEDNESDAY 2

THURSDAY 3

FRIDAY ◖ 4

SATURDAY 5

SUNDAY FATHER'S DAY (AUS/NZ) 6

SEPTEMBER 2026

MONDAY LABOR DAY (US) / LABOUR DAY (CAN) **7**

TUESDAY **8**

WEDNESDAY **9**

THURSDAY **10**

FRIDAY PATRIOT DAY (US) ○ **11**

SATURDAY **12**

SUNDAY GRANDPARENTS' DAY (US) **13**

The park has more than 300 glaciers—more than 8 times the number of glaciers in Glacier National Park!

SEPTEMBER 2026

MONDAY 14

TUESDAY FIRST DAY OF NATIONAL HISPANIC HERITAGE MONTH 15

WEDNESDAY 16

THURSDAY 17

FRIDAY ◗ **18**

SATURDAY **19**

SUNDAY YOM KIPPUR (BEGINS AT SUNSET) **20**

Many of the park's mountains have ominous names—
Mounts Terror, Fury, Despair, and Torment,
for example.

SEPTEMBER 2026

MONDAY 21

TUESDAY FALL EQUINOX 22

WEDNESDAY 23

THURSDAY 24

FRIDAY

25

SATURDAY ●

26

SUNDAY

27

More than 20 percent of Seattle's power requirements are supplied by the Ross Lake Dam within the park.

OCTOBER
Glacier National Park

Discover winter year-round at Glacier National Park. This park, established in 1886, is home to the famous Going-to-the-Sun Road, a stunning mountainside road that faces Going-to-the-Sun Mountain, a 9,647-foot mountain peak. The road itself can become blanketed in up to 80 feet of snow in the wintertime in an event called the Big Drift. Relatively few roads exist within Glacier National Park to preserve its beauty. In fact, it is a distinguished beauty: Waterton Lakes National Park and Glacier National Park together protect the incredible glacier-carved landscape known as the Crown of the Continent. In the summertime, enjoy

blooms of wildflowers at lower elevations. Hike the wheelchair-accessible Trail of the Cedars or take a tour of Lake McDonald in a handcrafted wooden boat. Trek over Avalanche Gorge to reach the reflective, glacial Avalanche Lake. And if you need a break from countless beautiful hikes, ride through the park in a vintage Red Jammer, the classic Glacier mode of transport since 1936. With 34 percent of the park's glaciers having already melted between 1966 and 2015, plan a visit to these magnificent glacial lakes, alpine meadows, and ice-covered peaks while you still can!

OCTOBER 2026

NOTES	SUNDAY	MONDAY	TUESDAY
		4	5	6
		LABOUR DAY (AUS-ACT/NSW/SA)	
	11	12	13
		INDIGENOUS PEOPLES' DAY (US) COLUMBUS DAY (US) THANKSGIVING DAY (CAN)	
	◗ 18	19	20
	25 ●	26	27
		LABOUR DAY (NZ)	

OCTOBER 2026

WEDNESDAY	THURSDAY	FRIDAY	SATURDAY
		1	2	3
		SIMCHAT TORAH (BEGINS AT SUNDOWN)	
7	8	9 ○	10
14	15	16	17
21	22	23	24
28	29	30	31 HALLOWEEN

GLACIER NATIONAL PARK

LOCATION: Northwestern Montana, on the border between Canada and the US

SIZE: 1,013,332 acres

BEST TIME TO VISIT: June through September

NATURE: Glacier boasts more than 1,100 species of vascular plants, such as aspen, butterwort, Douglas fir, glacier lilies, mountain maples, Pacific yew, and paper birch.

HABITATS: The park is home to more than 350 species of vertebrates, including the Canadian lynx, harlequin duck, long-toed salamander, pika, Rocky Mountain goat, and wolverine.

ACTIVITIES: Auto touring, biking, boating, camping, cross-country skiing, fishing, hiking, photography, and whitewater rafting.

NATURAL FEATURES: Avalanche Lake, Deadwood Falls, Grinnell Glacier, Haystack Creek, Iceberg Lake, Jackson Glacier, Logan Pass, The Garden Wall, and Virginia Falls.

SEPTEMBER/OCTOBER

MONDAY (SEPTEMBER)   **28**

TUESDAY (SEPTEMBER)   **29**

WEDNESDAY (SEPTEMBER)   **30**

THURSDAY   **1**

FRIDAY   SIMCHAT TORAH (BEGINS AT SUNDOWN)   **2**

SATURDAY ◖   **3**

SUNDAY   **4**

OCTOBER 2026

MONDAY LABOUR DAY (AUS-ACT/NSW/SA)   **5**

TUESDAY   **6**

WEDNESDAY   **7**

THURSDAY   **8**

FRIDAY   **9**

SATURDAY ○   **10**

SUNDAY   **11**

Triple Divide Peak sends water to the Atlantic, Arctic, and Pacific oceans at once.

OCTOBER 2026

MONDAY   INDIGENOUS PEOPLES' DAY (US) / COLUMBUS DAY (US) /
THANKSGIVING DAY (CAN)

12

TUESDAY

13

WEDNESDAY

14

THURSDAY

15

FRIDAY

16

SATURDAY

17

SUNDAY ◗

18

After visiting the park, venture 15 minutes to Whitefish, named one of the "Top 25 Ski Towns in the World" by NATIONAL GEOGRAPHIC.

OCTOBER 2026

MONDAY   **19**

TUESDAY   **20**

WEDNESDAY   **21**

THURSDAY   **22**

FRIDAY 23

SATURDAY 24

SUNDAY 25

Glacier National Park annually sees around 3 million visitors, which is almost triple the entire population of Montana.

NOVEMBER
Canyonlands National Park

There is no name more fitting than Canyonlands for a park that seems like a science-fiction, canyon-covered planet. Established in 1964 and located a mere 26 miles from Arches National Park, Canyonlands is the perfect escape for hikers, stargazers, and desert lovers. This park was carved by the powerful Green and Colorado Rivers, erosive streams that spread canyons like veins through the desert rock. The rivers divide the park into 3 districts—the popular and accessible Island in the Sky district, the wild and remote Maze district, and the Needles district, which is full of colorful sandstone spires. The park also includes a separate

Horseshoe Canyon, an archeological trove of pictographs and petroglyphs that can be explored on a steep 7-mile hike. Take in glowing sunrises at the White Rim Overlook or Shafer Trail Overlook, gaze up at the orange sandstone of Mesa Arch, or explore the enigmatic Upheaval Dome—this massive crater is a geological mystery, speculated to be caused by meteorite impact or a salt dome. In Canyonlands, you will experience some of the country's clearest skies; visitors can see up to 15,000 stars at night. Spend your days under an expanse of vibrant blue and fall asleep under the twinkling, boundless cosmos.

NOVEMBER 2026

NOTES	SUNDAY	MONDAY	TUESDAY
	◐ 1	2	3
	ALL SAINTS' DAY		
	8 ○	9	10
			ELECTION DAY (US)
	15	16 ◗	17
	22	23 ●	24
	29	30	

NOVEMBER 2026

WEDNESDAY	THURSDAY	FRIDAY	SATURDAY
4	5	6	7
11 VETERANS DAY (US)	12	13	14
18	19	20	21
25	26 THANKSGIVING DAY (US)	27 NATIVE AMERICAN HERITAGE DAY (US)	28

CANYONLANDS NATIONAL PARK

LOCATION: Southeastern Utah

SIZE: 337,598 acres

BEST TIME TO VISIT: March through October

NATURE: Canyonlands is home to more than 600 different plant species, such as columbine, maidenhair fern, netleaf hackberry, primrose, sand verbena, and tamarisk.

HABITATS: The park boasts almost 350 species of vertebrates, including the desert cottontail, humpback chub, kangaroo rat, razorback sucker, and yellow rattlesnake.

ACTIVITIES: Auto touring, backpacking, biking, boating, camping, climbing, hiking, horseback riding, and stargazing.

NATURAL FEATURES: Candlestick Tower, Green River, Horseshoe Canyon, Mesa Arch, Monument Basin, Shafer Canyon, and the Upheaval Dome.

OCTOBER/NOVEMBER

MONDAY (OCTOBER) LABOUR DAY (NZ) ●   **26**

TUESDAY (OCTOBER)   **27**

WEDNESDAY (OCTOBER)   **28**

THURSDAY (OCTOBER)   **29**

FRIDAY (OCTOBER)   **30**

SATURDAY (OCTOBER) HALLOWEEN   **31**

SUNDAY ALL SAINTS' DAY ◗   **1**

NOVEMBER 2026

MONDAY 2

TUESDAY 3

WEDNESDAY 4

THURSDAY 5

FRIDAY 6

SATURDAY 7

SUNDAY 8

*A large part of Canyonlands's soil is cryptobiotic crust,
a living soil made up of algae, bacteria, and lichens.*

NOVEMBER 2026

MONDAY ◯ **9**

TUESDAY ELECTION DAY (US) **10**

WEDNESDAY VETERANS DAY (US) **11**

THURSDAY **12**

FRIDAY 13

SATURDAY 14

SUNDAY 15

The Maze and the Needles districts are very remote
and only see about 3 percent of Canyonlands's visitors.

NOVEMBER 2026

MONDAY 16

TUESDAY ☽ 17

WEDNESDAY 18

THURSDAY 19

FRIDAY 20

SATURDAY 21

SUNDAY 22

127 HOURS, starring James Franco, is based on the true story of Aron Ralston, a climber who had to amputate his own arm after being trapped in a canyon slot in Canyonlands.

NOVEMBER 2026

MONDAY   **23**

TUESDAY ●   **24**

WEDNESDAY   **25**

THURSDAY   THANKSGIVING DAY (US)   **26**

FRIDAY NATIVE AMERICAN HERITAGE DAY (US)   **27**

SATURDAY   **28**

SUNDAY   **29**

In the Old West, Butch Cassidy's Wild Bunch had a hideout called Robbers Roost, which was located in the Maze district.

DECEMBER
Katmai National Park

Snowcapped peaks, sockeye salmon, and grizzly bears—legendary Alaskan wilderness is distilled into the cold but captivating Katmai National Park. This park, established in 1918, was created to protect the volcanically devastated land surrounding super volcano Novarupta, including its Valley of Ten Thousand Smokes and the fourteen active volcanoes in the area. The Katmai caldera was created after a record-breaking eruption in 1912. The natural disaster made the air so thick with ash that those in surrounding areas could not see a lantern held an arm's length away. Today, Katmai holds international appeal as home to the

world's largest known concentration of grizzly bears. In the summertime, stand on the famous Brooks Falls Platform to see some of Katmai's 2,000 grizzlies feast on salmon for the winter. Hike the Cultural Site Trail to learn about the Alaska Peninsula and to visit the site of a 4,000-year-old native village, or see the ashy Valley of Ten Thousand Smokes up close by trekking to the stunning Windy Creek Overlook and Ukak Falls. Katmai provides the chance to explore one of the most volcanically active and visually fascinating landscapes in the world—so what are you waiting for?

DECEMBER 2026

NOTES	SUNDAY	MONDAY	TUESDAY
			◑ 1
			WORLD AIDS DAY
	6	7	8
	13	14	15
	20	21	22
		WINTER SOLSTICE	
	27	28	29

DECEMBER 2026

WEDNESDAY	THURSDAY	FRIDAY	SATURDAY
2	**3**	**4**	**5**
	INTERNATIONAL DAY OF PERSONS WITH DISABILITIES	HANUKKAH (BEGINS AT SUNDOWN)	
○ **9**	**10**	**11**	**12**
	HUMAN RIGHTS DAY		
16 ☽	**17**	**18**	**19**
23 ●	**24**	**25**	**26**
			BOXING DAY (UK/CAN/AUS/NZ)
	CHRISTMAS EVE	CHRISTMAS DAY	FIRST DAY OF KWANZAA
☾ **30**	**31**		
	NEW YEAR'S EVE		

KATMAI NATIONAL PARK

....

LOCATION: Southern Alaska

SIZE: 4,093,077 acres

BEST TIME TO VISIT: June through September

NATURE: Katmai boasts more than 700 species of plants, including beachhead iris, fireweed, labrador tea, lowbush cranberry, monkshood, and watermelon berries.

HABITATS: The park is home to almost 200 species of vertebrates, such as the beluga whale, caribou, harbor seal, killer whale, lynx, river otter, and sockeye salmon.

ACTIVITIES: Bear watching, boating, camping, fishing, flightseeing, hiking, hunting, and photography.

NATURAL FEATURES: Brooks Falls, Hallo Bay, Mount Katmai, Novarupta, Naknek Lake, the Valley of Ten Thousand Smokes, and Ukak Falls.

NOVEMBER/DECEMBER

MONDAY (NOVEMBER)   **30**

TUESDAY   WORLD AIDS DAY   ◗   **1**

WEDNESDAY   **2**

THURSDAY   INTERNATIONAL DAY OF PERSONS WITH DISABILITIES   **3**

FRIDAY   HANUKKAH (BEGINS AT SUNDOWN)   **4**

SATURDAY   **5**

SUNDAY   **6**

DECEMBER 2026

MONDAY 7

TUESDAY 8

WEDNESDAY ○ 9

THURSDAY HUMAN RIGHTS DAY 10

FRIDAY 11

SATURDAY 12

SUNDAY 13

Katmai bears gorge themselves on salmon in preparation for winter, and the park's annual "Fat Bear Week" is a bracket-style competition in which voters crown a favorite fat bear.

DECEMBER 2026

MONDAY   **14**

TUESDAY   **15**

WEDNESDAY   **16**

THURSDAY ☽   **17**

FRIDAY 18

SATURDAY 19

SUNDAY 20

In 1923, Katmai National Park saw 15 visitors—and in 2019, its peak year, 84,167 people visited the park!

DECEMBER 2026

MONDAY WINTER SOLSTICE   **21**

TUESDAY   **22**

WEDNESDAY   **23**

THURSDAY CHRISTMAS EVE   **24**

FRIDAY CHRISTMAS DAY

25

SATURDAY BOXING DAY (UK/CAN/AUS/NZ) / FIRST DAY OF KWANZAA

26

SUNDAY

27

The Great Eruption of 1912, from Novarupta, was the largest volcanic eruption of the twentieth century and created the Katmai caldera.

DECEMBER 2026

MONDAY   **28**

TUESDAY   **29**

WEDNESDAY   **30**

THURSDAY NEW YEAR'S EVE   **31**

NOTES

NOTES

NOTES

NOTES

NOTES

NOTES

NOTES

First published in 2025 by Rock Point, an imprint of The Quarto Group,
142 West 36th Street, 4th Floor, New York, NY 10018, USA
(212) 779-4972 www.Quarto.com

Rock Point titles are also available at discount for retail, wholesale, promotional, and bulk purchase. For details, contact the Special Sales Manager by email at specialsales@quarto.com or by mail at The Quarto Group, Attn: Special Sales Manager, 100 Cummings Center Suite 265D, Beverly, MA 01915 USA.

10 9 8 7 6 5 4 3 2 1

ISBN: 978-1-57715-507-2

Group Publisher: Rage Kindelsperger
Editorial Director: Erin Canning
Creative Director: Laura Drew
Managing Editor: Cara Donaldson
Editor: Katelynn Abraham
Editorial Assistant: Alyana Nurani
Cover and Interior Design: Beth Middleworth
Book Layout: Danielle Smith-Boldt
Interior Illustrations by Aloysius Patrimonio with exception of the following pages: 14-15, 40-41, 228-229
Back Cover Illustration: Aloysius Patrimonio

Printed in China

This book provides general information on national parks and their inspirational and holistic benefits. However, it should not be relied upon as recommending or promoting any specific diagnosis or method of treatment for a particular condition, and it is not intended as a substitute for medical advice or for direct diagnosis and treatment of a medical condition by a qualified physician. Readers who have questions about a particular condition, possible treatments for that condition, or possible reactions from the condition or its treatment should consult a physician or other qualified healthcare professional.

All Moon phases shown are for the Eastern Time Zone.